Choosing, Planting and Cultivating Herbs

Choosing, Planting and Cultivating Herbs

by Philippa Back

illustrated by Linda Diggins

Keats Publishing, Inc. New Canaan, Connecticut

CHOOSING, PLANTING AND CULTIVATING HERBS

Published in 1977 by Keats Publishing, Inc.
by arrangement with
Darton, Longman and Todd, Ltd.
London, England

ISBN: 0-87983-149-9

Library of Congress Catalog Card Number 76-587-70

Printed in the United States of America

Keats Publishing, Inc.
36 Grove Street, New Canaan, Connecticut 06840

Contents

APPRECIATION 7

1. CHOOSING THE HERBS 9
The best herbs to grow in small gardens and their
yield for selling

2. PLANNING THE HERB GARDEN 14
Planning the herb garden with suggested layouts; herb beds; herbs in containers; wall
boxes, hanging baskets, window boxes, indoors

3. ALPHABETICAL LIST OF HERBS giving cultiva- 30
tion notes

4. GENERAL CULTIVATION 49
Details of cultivation; garden plot, patio plants,
window boxes, indoors; preparation; planting,
propagation, management, pests and diseases

5. HARVESTING, DRYING AND STORING 68

6. MARKETING AND OUTLETS   76
Marketing – pot-grown herbs, cut fresh herbs,
dried herbs and other products; outlets – local
shops, market stalls; health food shops, road-
side stands and herbal suppliers. How to pre-
pare a herb tea

7. ALPHABETICAL LIST OF HERBS giving the uses of   84
each plant

LIST OF BOOKS FOR FURTHER READING   94

Appreciation

Claire Loewenfeld was a well-known author and authority on the subject of herbs. For many years Mrs Loewenfeld undertook research work on herbs and during the war she pioneered the use of rosehips as a valuable source of vitamin C.

With her husband, Dr Gunther Loewenfeld, a horticulturist, Claire started Chiltern Herb Farms in Hertfordshire. Together they perfected the first English aromatic green-dried herbs and began to market them. A wide range of culinary herbs was offered and this included many fragrant flowers and leaves for herbal tisanes. Claire Loewenfeld was a warm and generous person.

When I joined her team at the Herb Farm in 1960 it was the beginning of a long and happy association which continued until her death in 1974. She was an excellent teacher and during those years I was fortunate enough to learn a great deal from her. I shall always remember Claire with affection and for the help she gave me and her willingness to share her knowledge. Dr Loewenfeld with his practical skill and extensive experience in the growing and marketing of herbs is one of very few in his field.

From him I have gained a further store of knowledge which has been invaluable to me. I am particularly grateful to Dr Loewenfeld for his inspiration which did so much to create this book, and to him I extend my warm appreciation and gratitude.

I

Choosing the Herbs

Herbs are in fashion, as evidenced by the many new books and articles written about them, by the increase of specialist herb shops, and even by the new concern for more natural medicines to avoid the over-use of modern drugs. The demand for herbs of every kind is growing – so why not grow herbs for profit?

Nearly everyone who has a garden, however small, grows some parsley, mint and chives for the kitchen, but even if you have never grown any herbs, they are easy to cultivate and make few demands on your time or available space.

Growing herbs to sell could become a profitable occupation or side line for the amateur gardener or the complete beginner, and especially for retired people keen on gardening, who could combine the pleasures with the added incentive of some income from the sales.

Herb growing and selling can be an all-the-year-round business if you own a greenhouse; the herbs can be sold either cut fresh in season, in pots for other growers and gardeners; green-dried in jars or bags. This means that surplus crops can always be used, for herbs must be cut at the right time, usually before flowering.

You could succeed with more specialised sales such as large crops of thyme, sage or marjoram for supplying to local butchers and sausage makers, who use these herbs in fairly large quantities. Your best plan would be to dry the herbs at home and crush them for packing into containers, which should be made of glass or plastic with screw-top lids. You could then come to an arrangement with your buyer to return the empties for re-use.

Dried herbs keep best if not exposed to light, so the jars will need a large masking label and these can be an attractive selling feature, perhaps especially printed with your name on them.

There are herbs for many different purposes. The main group is for cooking. Some of them are known and used regularly by the public; others are seldom grown or sold but are nevertheless wonderful flavouring herbs, used for centuries on the continent.

Familiar kitchen herbs

Parsley	Thyme	Rosemary
Mint	Garlic	Marjoram
Chives	Basil	Tarragon
Sage	Dill	Fennel

Less known flavours

Chervil	Summer Savory	Caraway
Lemon Balm	Sweet Cicely	Coriander
Salad Burnet	Welsh Onion	Lovage

Herbs for special purposes

There are also herbs which can be used for summer drinks, cake decorations and jam making.

Angelica	Bowles Mint	Marigold
Anise	Coriander	Nasturtium
Borage	Peppermint	Rose Geranium

Herbs in winter

Some herbs are suitable for growing indoors or in a green-house to give a fresh supply in winter.

Parsley
Chives
Chervil (seeds to be sown in autumn)
Dill (seeds to be sown in autumn)

Fragrant herbs for gifts

Many specialist herb shops, gift shops and counters now sell a wide variety of fragrant products suitable for present giving; old-fashioned ideas revived such as lavender bags, herb sachets and pot-pourris. These too can be made at home then sold fresh or pre-dried:

Angelica	Costmary	Lemon Verbena
Anise	Dill	Peppermint
Basil	Eau de Cologne Mint	Rose Geranium
Bergamot	Lavender	Rosemary
Borage	Lemon Balm	Sage
Bowles Mint	Lemon Thyme	Tarragon
Coriander		

Pot-pourris

Some of the flowers needed for petals to provide scent and colour to the mixtures will already be growing in the garden.

Chamomile flowers	Pansies
Cornflowers	Roses
Marigold petals	Verbascum flowers
Nasturtium flowers	

Should you decide to specialise in any of the suggested groups of herbs it is advisable to start by growing just a few of as many varieties as possible. In this way you will discover which herbs do best in your locality and in your garden, both from the selling and cultivation points of view. Once your herb plants and your reputation are established you can gradually start to specialise in the herb group of your choice.

Some herbs, the annuals, have to be sown and can be started in boxes or pots in the greenhouse, in cold frames or under cloches for later transplanting. Otherwise, the seeds are sown at the appropriate time in their permanent positions in the herb garden or beds, and thinned out.

Herbs for sowing

Anise	Chervil	Parsley
Basil	Coriander	Summer Savory
Borage	Dill	Sweet Marjoram
Caraway	Garlic (bulblets)	

Flowers for sowing

Chamomile	Nasturtium
Cornflowers	Pansies
Marigold	Verbascum

Herbs to be planted

Other herbs, the perennials and biennials, can be bought as plants from herb nurseries – as the seeds are not always easy to obtain.

Angelica	Lemon Verbena	Sweet Cicely
Chives	Lovage	Tarragon
Costmary	Mints	Thyme
Fennel	Pot Marjoram	Welsh Onion
Hyssop	Sage	
Lemon Balm	Salad Burnet	

Herb shrubs

And some herbs are shrubs or trees which are also obtainable from general nurseries.

| Bay | Rose Geranium |
| Lavender | Rosemary |

Having put into groups the best herbs for the purpose, it should be stressed that you do not need to have a garden in order to cultivate and sell your herbs. Many of the herbs listed can be grown in containers of one kind or another. You only need to consult the alphabetical list of herbs on p. 30 to realise that a variety of herbs can be grown in this way.

The whole idea of growing and selling your own herbs is open to flat dwellers with space on their window sills both inside and out, and may be followed by those whose town garden consists of a small backyard, a patio, three bare walls or just a balcony. Here you can accommodate herbs in tubs, boxes and large pots as well as many other types of plant holders. Provided they meet the basic requirements set out in this book, the choice of container is left to you.

Lastly there are other advantages in growing herbs which are quite apart from any monetary profit you may make.

You will find you get much pleasure from your herbs with their beautiful leaves and flowers, and their heady scents. When you pass by a plant touching the leaves you will immediately be surrounded by its lovely perfume. One or two of the stronger herbs have an almost exotic scent. You will be able to try out the various herbs in your cooking, adding new tastes to old established dishes, and discovering how each plant has its own unique flavour.

You can enjoy making gifts for friends or family using your own fragrant herbs. A bunch of sweet smelling herbs is one of the nicest gifts to give to a blind person, who will get such pleasure from the many different scents.

2

Planning the Herb Garden

One great advantage in planning a herb garden is that there are so many different forms it can take. This gives you a wide choice and you can use as much or as little space as you wish. The size can vary from the semi-formal bed through the herb flanked paths and sloping banks to the containers and humble window box. The large formal herb gardens were originally cultivated by the religious orders of monks. They used culinary and healing herbs to add flavour to other edible plants and meats, and to treat the sick.

The herb beds were carefully designed, often following the pattern of the cloisters of a monastery. The whole garden was usually enclosed by hedges or walls and the beds, sometimes raised, were interspersed with trim paths.

The physic gardens of the fourteenth and fifteenth centuries were planted with medicinal herbs. These were carefully tended and jealously guarded. Knowledge of the plants and for which ailment each would be used, was handed down the generations through the mistress of the household.

The best known design for a formal herb garden is the 'knot garden', popular during Elizabethan times. Low growing herbs were chosen to emphasise their contrasting leaf colours and textures. They were planted in lines neatly interlaced one with another to give the appearance of a knotted rope (see Diagram 1).

Such a garden was fragrant and lovely to look at but required much time and work to maintain it. Nowadays this complicated design of a large herb garden is not really a practical proposition. Nevertheless when you are starting a garden and intend to sell your herbs, there are certain factors which have to be considered, making a plan necessary.

Diagram 1

The aspect of the herb bed is of primary importance. The large majority of herbs originally came from the Mediterranean region where the climate is sunny and the soil rather dry and poor. Your herb bed should ideally face south or west. It should be emphasised that though most herbs do not require a rich soil they will be subjected to constant cutting. The soil will therefore need to be of better substance than that in their native habitats.

It is not always easy to find such an ideal site in a small garden but a compromise can usually be made. Provided the herbs can be protected from the north and east and will get some sunshine during the day, the plants should flourish. You need to put your growing area to the best possible use. Your aim should be to combine utility with simplicity and pleasure.

At this stage you should decide in what form you intend to sell your herbs – as dried, fresh cut sprigs or pot-grown plants. Then choose the various plants you would like to grow. Take into consideration those herbs that will prosper in your soil as well as those most likely to be in demand in your district.

Include a selection of the more popular herbs like chives, parsley and sage, for they will be easy to sell. Choose also some which may be used in pot-pourris and sachets as well as in cooking. They would include rosemary, costmary and lemon thyme. You would then have a double market for these herbs.

You should work out the total growing area available to you and calculate the number of herbs you will be able to get into that space. Remember to take into account the diameter of the plant when fully grown. The herb bed may look a bit sparse to begin with but if you overfill it, the plants will become leggy and weak and the flavours will suffer as a result. Some of this extra space may usefully be employed in the growing of annuals during the early years in the development of your herb garden.

Do not plant fennel and dill side by side in your herb bed unless you are careful not to allow either plant to go into flower. Cross-pollination will take place and produce seeds and leaves which are neither one nor the other. If you keep the flower stems of tall-growing herbs cut back they will not overwhelm other plants growing nearby. On the other hand the taller plants can be used to shade smaller herbs where necessary.

You can work out from the cultivation chart the best position of each herb you choose to grow, then make your plan accordingly – perhaps following one of the designs suggested.

Paths are important in these designs and are not wasted space. They ensure that every plant comes within manageable reach. You must be able to reach each herb easily when picking it without trampling over other plants. Paths should be of brick, paving stones, gravel or concrete slabs. Grass paths are unsuitable because being narrow they are difficult to mow and the edges need constant clipping if the grass is not to wander amongst the herbs.

You will need to take into account the width of your paths in your plan. Main paths should be about $2\frac{1}{2}$ ft. wide. The smaller ones need only be 18 ins. wide – the width of a paving-stone or concrete slab.

Bricks make a very attractive path. Each brick is 9 ins. long and $4\frac{1}{4}$ ins. wide, so two bricks laid end to end or four laid side by side will be sufficiently wide for a path. Other patterns for a path such as herringbone or basketweave pattern can be followed if wished. Bricks are more easily laid on to a layer of sand. Leave a narrow gap between each brick to fill with mortar – to prevent weeds.

When choosing bricks for your paths, select a soft red or multi-coloured brick which will withstand frost. Second-hand red bricks when available can provide variations of colour and texture which blend well with plants and soil.

Paving stones of different shapes and sizes may also be laid on to sand or on to a weak cement–lime–sand mix ($1 : 1 : 6$). This may be purchased pre-mixed in bags, needing only the addition of water.

Suggested layouts for herbs

A semi-formal herb bed is an easy way to keep your herb plants looking neat and tidy. It comprises one long and two small sections divided by paths. The size is about 10 ft. long and 8 ft. wide, but can be adapted to your own requirements (Diagram 2).

You could plant one section of the bed with all perennials and another with annuals. Some herbs, such as bay or rosemary, grow rather slowly; you should therefore start with two or three plants of each. Restrict the roots of mint and tarragon by putting pieces of slate or tile, edge downwards all round the plant.

Annuals can be planted close together so they will sup-

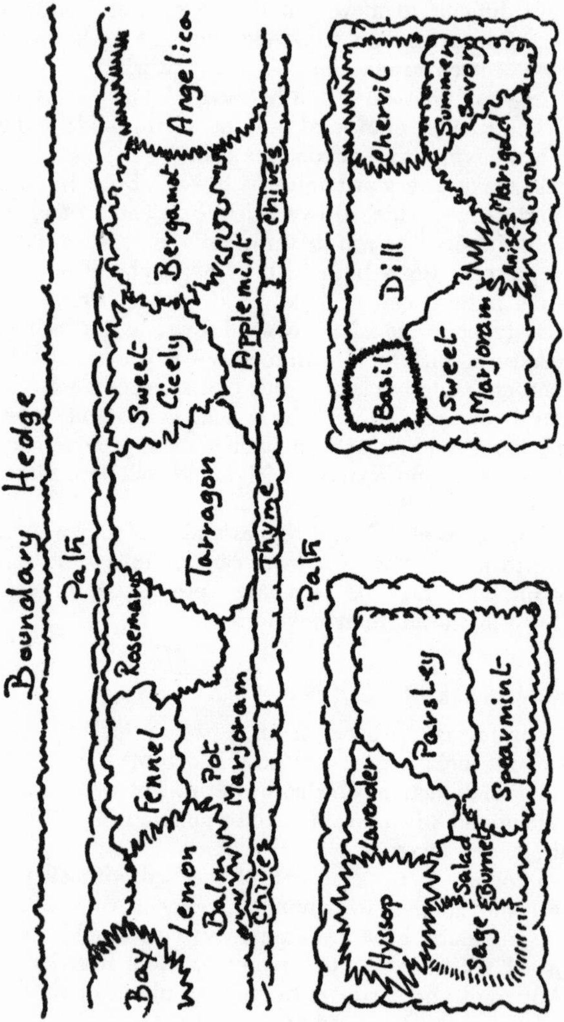

Boundary Hedge

Path

Bay · Lemon Balm · Fennel · Rosemary · Pot Marjoram · Tarragon · Sweet Cicely · Bergamot · Angelica

Chives

Path

Thyme · Applemint · Chives

Hyssop · Lavender · Sage · Salad Burnet · Parsley · Spearmint

Basil · Sweet Marjoram · Dill · Chervil · Sweet Savory · Summer Savory · Pot Marigold

Diagram 2

18

port each other. When thinning the young plants, leave 6 ins. between seedlings. Leave the same distance when putting out bought plants.

Do not be afraid of planting up a partly shaded bed with herbs. There are a number of shade-loving herbs which will flourish. Choose herbs such as chervil, spearmint, peppermint, bergamot and sweet cicely.

The round bed with its five small sections each surrounded by a path is roughly 9 ft. in diameter. It could be placed as a feature in the centre of a small garden (Diagram 3).

Use the same plan for a smaller diameter raised bed on a patio – the bed must be at least 12 ins. high – and omit the paths. Instead put bricks or pieces of paving slab amongst the herbs so that you can reach every plant.

This perennial bed is about 4 ft. by $2\frac{1}{2}$ ft. If you have sufficient space to have a small herb bed tucked away in a corner of the garden, plant it with evergreen herbs and shrubs only. Useful for constant picking throughout the winter, the plants can otherwise be left alone to become firmly established. A good selection of both culinary and pot-pourris herbs can be grown in such a bed (Diagram 4).

Narrow herb beds each about 15 ft. long and $2\frac{1}{2}$ ft. wide bordering a garden path near the house can make an attractive show. The edging plants of thyme and winter savory can come into their own here. Choose other low growing plants and have plenty of variety so that you can continue cutting throughout the year (Diagram 5).

The lavender hedge at the back of one border and sage at the back of the other make good backgrounds for the smaller herbs. Other good hedging plants are hyssop and rosemary. Hyssop grows quickly so early clipping to keep it bushy will be necessary. Rosemary is best placed entirely on its own, it grows rather slowly and needs more space than other hedging plants. Once established however, it provides excellent shelter for the garden. Use rosemary to hide the compost heap, shelter a windy spot in the garden or as a neat hedge flanking a pathway.

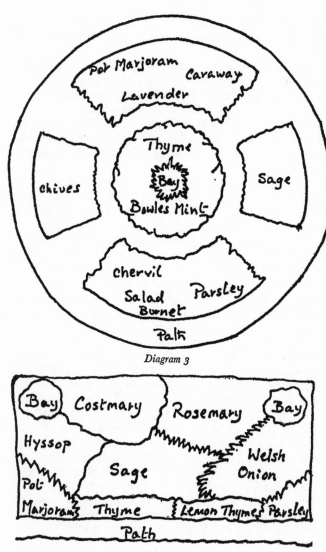

Pot Marjoram Caraway
Lavender
Thyme
Bay
Bowles Mint
Chives
Sage
Chervil
Salad Burnet
Parsley
Path

Diagram 3

Bay Costmary Rosemary Bay
Hyssop Welsh Onion
Pot Marjoram Sage Thyme Lemon Thyme Parsley
Path

Diagram 4

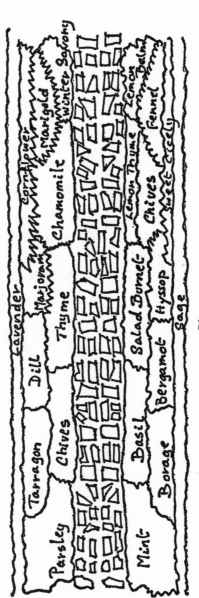

Diagram 5

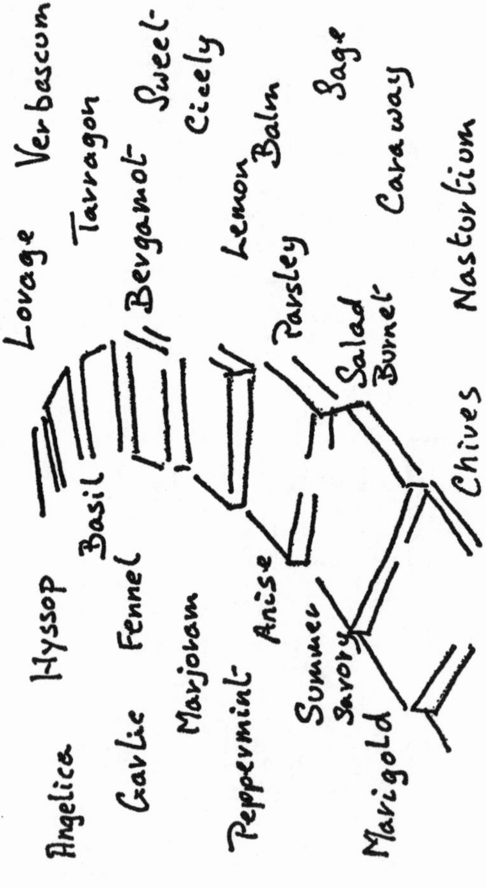

Angelica Hyssop Lovage Verbascum

Garlic Fennel Tarragon

Marjoram Basil Bergamot Sweet-Cicely

Peppermint- Anise Lemon Balm

Parsley Sage

Summer Savory Salad Burnet Caraway

Marigold Chives Nasturtium

Diagram 6

22

The selection of herb plants for growing on a gently sloping bank is easy if the bank faces south. The taller herbs should be placed at the top and sides of the bank to shelter the smaller ones in front. Where it is not possible easily to reach the individual herbs, place pieces of paving slab amongst them. Alternatively make a path to slant down the bank and tuck thyme plants in between the paving slabs. Where the bank is very steep it is advisable to terrace it, otherwise it is difficult to work and earth will constantly be washed down (Diagram 6).

In between the vegetables

In a small area of ground you can combine the growing of herbs with your vegetables. This scheme is especially suitable when selling pot-grown plants. The herbs are sown and grown in black polythene pots and these are sunk into the ground between rows of vegetables. You will need to make sure you are growing the most suitable herbs by studying their requirements and those of the vegetables. You will find that you cannot grow caraway in between rows of runner beans as the beans would soon be smothered by the caraway which grows very quickly. Nor can you count on the space between potato plants for they will need earthing up. However you can grow dill successfully between carrots and lettuces as these finish early. Marjoram will grow well between dwarf beans.

In some instances the plants help each other. A row of mint planted between young cabbages will lessen the incidence of whitefly on the cabbages. Summer savory planted amongst rows of broad beans will help to prevent an attack of blackfly.

This movable herb bed is suitable for inclusion in a patio design or where space is limited in a garden.

The plants are in plastic pots standing on a thick layer of gravel or sand – at least 2 ins. To keep the gravel and pots in position, surround them with one or two layers of bricks or piled up stones (Diagram 7).

Suggestions : 2 Coriander
2 Chives
2 Basil
2 Marjoram
2 Thyme
2 Savory

Diagram 7

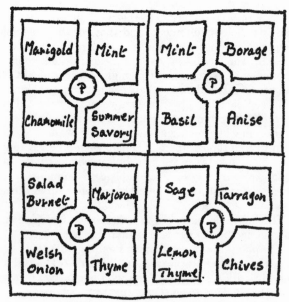

Marigold	Mint	Mint	Borage
Chamomile	Summer Savory	Basil	Anise
Salad Burnet	Marjoram	Sage	Tarragon
Welsh Onion	Thyme	Lemon Thyme	Chives

Centre of each block: Parsley

Diagram 8

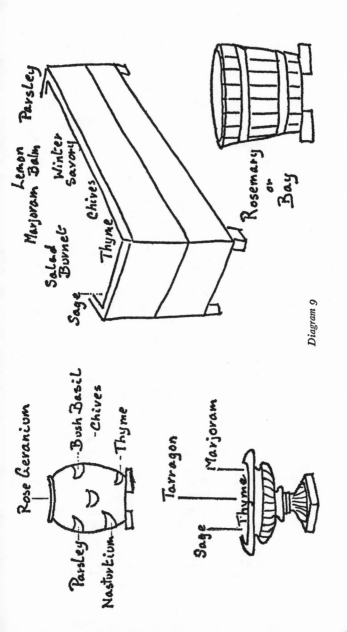

Rose Geranium

----Bush Basil

-Chives

-Thyme

Parsley

Nasturtium

Tarragon

Marjoram

Sage ----Thyme

Sage

Salad Burnet

Marjoram

Lemon Balm

Winter Savory

Chives

Thyme

Parsley

Rosemary or Bay

Diagram 9

It can be a help to be able to place the bed exactly where you need it, in the sun or shade and as large or as small as you wish to make it. It is easy to take up the plants when you are selling or renewing them. The plants will need frequent watering as there will be greater evaporation and no natural absorption of moisture from the ground.

A small herb bed can be quickly and easily made using four decorative concrete blocks, the kind that are usually sold to build garden windbreaks. They are usually about 18 ins. square. These are laid on their sides and sunk into the ground to half their depth. If used on a patio, take up the required number of paving slabs or bricks to let in the concrete blocks (Diagram 8).

Patio plants in containers. Use wooden troughs and tubs, stone urns and sinks, and flower pots of all shapes and sizes (Diagram 9).

If they are to remain in the same place for a great length of time the containers should be raised slightly from the ground to sit on bricks. Some containers can be bought with legs already attached.

Unglazed flower pots are inexpensive containers though large ones tend to take up more space than is necessary to provide growing area for the same number of herbs. Long wooden boxes and tubs make good containers with the added advantage that they can be moved indoors in the autumn.

A terracotta strawberry jar is an effective way of growing a variety of different herbs in a small area. The jars can be bought in various sizes from about one to three feet high. Each jar has from six to ten little pockets in which to plant the herbs. Grow a lovely scented rose geranium in the top. Chives, bush basil, summer savory and parsley can be grown in the lower pockets. In the bottom layer of pockets have the trailing herbs, thyme, marjoram, sage and nasturtium.

Strawberry jars together with other clay pots are very suitable for growing herbs on balconies.

Remember to keep the plants well watered as a great amount of moisture will evaporate through the pots. Never overfill a container with plants. As a rough guide, a wooden trough 4 ft. long, 12 ins. deep and 12 ins. wide will take ten herbs. A good selection would be two parsley plants and one each of marjoram, chives, winter savory, sage, lemon balm, garden thyme and salad burnet.

Rosemary is not suitable in a container with other plants but will grow well on its own in a tub, as will a bay tree.

The mints and tarragon are perhaps best on their own in containers because their roots spread so rapidly and encroach on other herbs growing nearby. If space does not allow this, set them in a bottomless pot within the container.

Where two or more plants are in one container, try to choose those herbs that need the same soil, the same amount of watering and sun or shade.

Plants between paving slabs

Many different herbs can be grown on a patio or in a backyard where every inch of space can and needs to be utilised. If the patio is paved it may be possible to lift one or two of the slabs. Fork up the soil or, if it seems sour, renew it altogether. Sink into these spaces plants which have shallow creeping roots; a lemon thyme, pot marjoram or lemon balm.

You can grow herbs successfully in boxes attached to a wall where these are suitable. On the brick walls of the house or garden or on a wooden fence provided it can support the necessary weight. The boxes can be obtained in various lengths.

Make sure the box sits on brackets firmly attached to the wall. If the box touches the wall there will be dirty marks down it when the water runs through the box.

Many herbs can be grown in wall boxes, they also save space and can look very attractive. The boxes should be placed at a height suitable to those who will tend them. They are ideal for those gardeners who find difficulty in stooping and for those confined to wheelchairs.

Wall boxes can also be obtained made out of plastic covered wire, light and easy to move if necessary. These could be hung on hooks attached to the wall and hold your herbs which are growing in their own polythene pots.

Hanging baskets or pots

To save further space in a small area use hanging baskets or pots – the pots must have drainage holes. Hang them from an iron bracket firmly attached to a wall or porch beam, provided it is not too high. The trailing herbs look best in this way; the thymes, nasturtium and marjoram. Even herbs such as basil and sage will start trailing as their stems grow longer. A hanging basket containing two or three different mints can look distinctive and smell delightful.

Be careful not to hang baskets one above the other. When the top one is watered drips will fall on the leaves of the lower plants causing staining, blotching or even rust disease – especially if the plants in the top basket have been watered with liquid feed.

Where plants are grown in an outside window box, the box can either be filled with earth and planted up or used to hold potted plants. If pots are standing on the window sill on their own they must be protected from falling by a retaining ledge.

The smaller herb plants are naturally the best ones to grow in a window box, but if you wish to have one or two of those which are likely to grow large, such as sage or costmary, plant them at the ends of the box and keep them compact by cutting. In this way the choice of herbs is wider; those most suitable are parsley, chives, thyme, marjoram, winter savory, bush basil, sage, nasturtium and salad burnet. Mint is best grown in its own pot, a window box is really unsuitable for its invasive roots. Keep the pot of mint standing in a saucer of water to maintain the moisture level in the pot.

Herbs grown continually indoors are best in their individual pots, rather than growing them together in a single container. The pots should stand on a thick layer of gravel or sand in a plastic or wooden pot tray, not less than 3 ins. in depth. It should always be kept watered but do not allow the water level to come to the top of the gravel. The evaporation from this water will help to keep the air round the herbs moist and prevent them from drying out too quickly. Once a week top up the box with liquid feed.

In the kitchen box of cooking herbs, a collection of five plants is suggested, marjoram, chives, bay, sage and thyme. Pots containing larger herb plants can be placed in other rooms in the house where suitable. These should stand on sand or gravel in saucers of water and be fed regularly.

The chart will suggest those herbs which do not need direct sunlight for good growth.

3

Alphabetical List of Herbs

giving Cultivation Notes

Angelica

Angelica
Archangelica

Biennial, re-seeds freely. Height to 6 ft. Moist rich soil. Part-shaded position at back of bed. Allow 2 ft. between plants and rows. 3–4 plants sufficient to start. Not suitable for containers. Sow seed immediately it ripens on flower head, about August. Take root cuttings in autumn.

Anise

Pimpinella anisum

Annual. Height to 2 ft. Light, rich soil. Grow in full sun. Sow seed in final position. Germination is 14–16 days. Thin seedlings to 6 ins. apart. Support plants when tall, by running string along each side of row.

Basil (sweet)

Ocimum basilicum

Delicate annual. Height 1–1½ ft. Moist, well-drained soil. Grow in full sun, sheltered position. Sow seed thinly under glass in February/March, outside in May. Slow to germinate. Plant out seedlings in June 8 ins. apart only – they support each other. Pinch out centres of plants to make stems stronger.

(Bush)

Annual. Height 6 ins. Grow in good potting compost in containers in sunny, sheltered position. Sow seed in pots in March. Thin to 2 plants per 4-in. pot. Keep centres pinched out to encourage bushy growth. Stand pots on gravel, water from the bottom.

Bay

Laurus nobilis

Perennial evergreen tree. Can grow to 40 ft. Clipping will keep it low. Very slow growing. Grow in ordinary garden soil. When established transplant to sunny position – 2nd or 3rd year. Protect from severe frost. Start with 3 or 4 plants. Take stem cuttings in autumn using half-ripe shoots. Good grown singly in pots or tubs. Can be brought indoors in winter.

Bergamot, Red

Monarda didyma

Hardy perennial, dies down in winter.
Height 2–3 ft. Fairly rich, moist soil.
Grows in sun or shade. Space plants 2 ft.
apart. Keep compact by cutting. Divide
annually by root division or take root cuttings in spring or autumn. Retain outer
shoots only – discard woody centre.

Borage

Borago officinalis

Annual, re-seeds freely. Height 1½–2 ft.
Grows in any soil fairly quickly. Reaches
maturity in 5–6 weeks. Goes on flowering
till frost. Allow 2 ft. between plants. Sow
seed in March, April and July for succession. Not suitable for containers because of long tap root.

An old fashioned herb garden
Scotney Castle, Kent

Herbs in an informal garden

Growing herbs in restricted spaces

A herb garden with formal lay-out
Sissinghurst Castle, Kent

Caraway

Carum carvi

Hardy biennial, will self-sow if some plants left uncut. Height to 2 ft. Well-drained soil, sunny position. Protect plants in severe winter. Sow seed in final growing position in April or October. Germinates quickly. Thin to 12 ins. apart.

Chamomile

Matricaria chamomilla

Annual variety is the 'true' chamomile. Height 1½ ft. Once germinated prefers dry, sunny position. Sow seed in spring or autumn, protect during winter. Germinates slowly. Thin plants to 9 ins. apart Pick flowers from May/September.

Chervil

Anthriscum cerifolium

Annual, will re-seed itself. Height 1–2 ft. Well-drained light, sandy soil. Partial shade at hottest time of day. Sow seed in August for 1st cutting in September and 2nd cutting in October. Sow from January onwards. Thin plants to 9 ins. apart. Grows well in containers. Suitable for indoor growing in light, not sunny, position. Allow 3 plants per 6-in. pot.

Chives

Allium schoenoprasum

Hardy perennial. Height to 10 ins. Fairly rich soil. Sunny or part-shaded position. Plants need feeding during growing season or tips of leaves go brown. Sow seed in spring. Germinates slowly. Thin to 12 ins. apart. Divide clumps in spring or autumn. Have 12–20 plants to start. In containers, plant in good potting compost. Use liquid feed every 14 days. Allow 2 plants per 6-in. pot.

Coriander

Coriandrum sativum

Annual. Height 1–1½ ft. Fairly rich but light soil. Sunny position. Sow seed in early spring in final growing position. Germinates quickly. Thin to 6 ins. apart. May need supporting. When seeds are ripe, cut plants and leave 2–3 days to complete ripening then thresh. Can be grown in containers but has unpleasant scent until seeds are ripe.

Cornflower

Centaurea cyanus

Hardy annual. Height to 2 ft. Any soil, sunny position. Sow seed from August/October for good bushy plants. Thin to 12 ins. apart in spring. Many flowers to each plant.

Costmary

Chrysanthemum balsamita

Hardy perennial. Height 2–3 ft. Any soil
sunny or part-shaded position. Set plants
12 ins. apart. Increase by root division in
spring or autumn.

Dill

Anethum graveolens or
Peucadanum graveolens

Annual. Height to 3 ft. In dry weather
tends to 'bolt' and go to seed unless
watered. Well-drained soil, sunny position. Sow seed in final growing position
from April/June. Allow 12–20 ins. between rows and 9 ins. between plants.
Start with a good number of plants.

Fennel

Foeniculum vulgare. var. dulce (sweet)
Foeniculum piperitum (Florence)

Hardy perennial, dies down in winter.
Sow seed in sunny spot in April/May, or
divide roots of existing plants. Start with
4–6 plants. Best renewed every 2–3 years.
Height 4–5 ft.

Garlic

Allium sativum

Hardy perennial. Height 1–3 ft. Rich soil,
sunny moist position. Plant garlic cloves
or bulblets 2 ins. deep and 8 ins. apart in
March or October. Flowers must be cut
off. Harvest when leaves die down before
winter sets in. Each plant produces one
bulb made up of many cloves.

Hyssop

Hyssopus officinalis

Hardy evergreen shrub. Height $1\frac{1}{2}$–2 ft.
Light, well-drained soil. Sunny position.
Sow seed in spring. Take stem cuttings in
spring or autumn. Set plants 12 ins. apart.
Suitable for container growing.

Lavender

Lavendula vera (English)
Lavendula dentala (French)

Perennial shrubby plant. Height $1\frac{1}{2}$–4 ft.
Sunny position in well-drained soil.
Becomes large and woody unless cut back
at end of each flowering season. Allow 12
ins. between dwarf varieties, 24 ins. between English. Sow seed in early spring
or take stem cuttings in spring or autumn.

Lemon Balm

Melissa officinalis

Hardy perennial. Height 1½–2 ft. Moist, rich soil in sunny or part-shaded position. Sow seed in March/April. Thin plants to 12 ins. apart. Divide plants in spring or autumn or take stem cuttings. Very easy to grow. Suitable for container growing.

Lemon Verbena

Lippia citriodora

Perennial deciduous shrub. Height to 2 ft. Best grown in pots under glass or indoors. In warm districts grow outside in poor soil in sheltered place. Divide plants in spring.

Lovage

Ligusticum officinalis or
Scotium

Perennial, dies down in winter. Height
5–7 ft. Any soil, moist position. Can be
raised from seed and transplanted to permanent site in autumn or spring. Allow 2
ft. between plants. Increase by root division in spring or autumn.

Marigold

Calendula officinalis

Annual, re-seeds itself. Height 18 ins. Any
soil, sunny position. Sow seed freely in
March/April. Thin to 12–18 ins. apart.

Marjoram (*sweet*)

Origanum majorana

Grown as annual. Height 10–12 ins. Bushy plant. Grow in full sun in moist fairly rich soil. Cannot usually stand frost. Sow seed under glass in spring. Plant out in May, 8 ins. apart. Germinates slowly.

Marjoram (*pot*)

Origanum onites

Perennial. Height to 2 ft. Creeping growth and roots. Sow seed in April in dry, light soil in warm position. Thin plants to 18 ins. apart. Divide plants in spring or autumn, discarding woody centres. Makes a good indoor plant.

Mint

Mentha viridis (spearmint)
Mentha rotundiflora (Bowles or apple mint)
Mentha citrata (Eau de Cologne mint)
Mentha piperita (peppermint)

All perennials and great spreaders. Heights are from $1\frac{1}{2}$–2 ft. Moist, rich soil, partial shade. Plant new shoots in spring or roots in autumn 9 ins. apart. All mints need roots restricted or they overgrow other herbs.

Nasturtium

Tropaeolum majus or minus

Annual, dwarf or climber, re-seeds itself. Height 1–8 ins. Germinates quickly. Flowers freely in poor soil and sunny position. Sow seed March/April. Space plants 12 ins. apart. If space limited choose dwarf varieties. Good for container growing.

Parsley

Petroselinum crispum (curly)
Petroselinum sativum (hamburg)

Biennial. Height 6–8 ins. Sunny or part-shaded position. Seeds slow to germinate, 5–8 weeks. Start sowing early in boxes or outside under cloches. Allow 8 ins. between plants, 12–18 ins. between rows. Cut often, do not allow to flower, to get maximum crops. Best in first year.

Rose Geranium

Pelargonium graveolens

Perennial shrub but not hardy. Dies after frost. Height 2 ft. Warm sheltered position. Light, sandy soil. Set plants 18–24 ins. apart in spring, or take stem cuttings in August. Bring indoors in winter. Suitable for container growing.

Rosemary

Rosemarinus officinalis

Perennial evergreen shrub. Height to 4ft. Light, sandy rather dry soil – needs lime. Sunny sheltered position. Very slow growing. Sow seed in April. Best to buy plants. Take stem cuttings, divide roots or layer side-shoots in May. Plants should finally have 3 ft. space all round. Can be kept compact by cutting. Excellent in containers and indoors.

Sage

Salvia officinalis

Perennial. Height to 2 ft. Easy to grow in dry sunny position. Sow seed in April and thin to 1½ ft. apart. Take stem cuttings in May. Becomes woody after 3–4 years when it should be divided and young roots replanted. Begin with 12 plants. Suitable for container growing and indoors.

Salad Burnet

Sanguisorba minor

Hardy perennial, will self-sow. Height
1–1½ ft. Very easy to grow. Well-drained
chalky soil in sunny position. Sow seed in
April in rows – allow 12 ins. between
them. Germinates quickly. Thin seedlings
to 6 ins. apart. Roots can be divided in
autumn. Good compact plant for container growing.

Summer Savory

Satureia hortensis

Annual. Height 12 ins. Moist rich soil, in
sunny position. Sow seed in April/May.
Thin seedlings to 12 ins apart. Can be
sown under glass in early spring. Suitable
for container growing.

Winter Savory

Satureia montana (Winter)

Hardy perennial. Height 6–12 ins. Poor
well-drained soil in full sun. Sow seed in
August/September or divide roots in
spring. Allow 15 ins. between plants.
Compact growing plant. Suitable for container growing and indoors.

Sweet Cicely

Myrrhis odorata

Perennial, dies down in winter, self-sows
freely. Height 3–5 ft. Well-drained soil,
partial shade. Best started from young
plants. Allow 18 ins. between mature
plants. Needs continuous removal of
flowers during season.

Tarragon

Artemesia dracunculus (French)
A. draconculoides (Russian)

Perennial. Height to 2 ft. Well-drained
dry soil in sunny position. Allow 18 ins.
between plants. Start by buying 6 plants.
Appears in April to harvest all through
growing season. Divide plants every 3–4
years.

Russian tarragon easier to grow but
flavour not so good – better used fresh.
Roots should be restricted from growing
into other herbs.

Thyme

Thymus vulgaris
T. citriodorus (Lemon thyme)

Evergreen perennial – seeds itself. Height
4–12 ins. Dry well-drained soil – needs
lime. Sunny position. Start with plants
and allow 12–18 ins. between plants.
Take stem cuttings or divide plants
April/May. Layer side shoots in
March/April. Compact plant very suitable for container growing and indoors.

Verbascum

Verbascum thapsiforme
V. thapsus

Biennial. Height 4–5 ft. Any soil in a sunny sheltered position. Sow seed in August, transplant in October. Allow $1\frac{1}{2}$–2 ft. between plants.

Welsh Onion

Allium fistulosum

Hardy perennial. Height 12 ins. Rich well-drained soil in a sunny position. Sow seed in spring and autumn. Divide plants in April or September. Leaves can be cut throughout the year. Suitable for container growing and indoors.

4

General Cultivation

Garden Plot

To produce good quality well-flavoured herbs it is worth-while spending time and effort in preparation of the site.

Herbs will grow in almost any good garden soil but will be sturdier plants if grown in moist, well-drained loam.

This is the ideal garden soil which contains a balanced mixture of sand, clay, lime and humus or organic matter. It is free-draining, friable and easy to work. It warms up quickly in the spring so that herbs can be sown or planted out early in the season. Perennials will start coming into leaf sooner and your whole selling programme can be brought forward.

The aim therefore, is to convert your garden soil as far as possible into a good loam. It already contains the right ingredients – it is just a case of getting them into the right proportions.

Know Your Soil

CHALK   This has only a few inches of dark top soil. The subsoil is white with lumps of chalk. Drainage is usually good but top soil can get wet and sticky after pro-longed rain.

CLAY OR HEAVY LOAM   Smooth shiny soil which sticks

together in lumps in winter and becomes rock hard in summer when dried out.

PEAT   Soil is black or dark brown and has a spongy texture. Easily becomes waterlogged.

SANDY   Gritty soil, light, crumbly and porous. Dries out quickly due to open texture.

STONY   More than 30–40 large and small stones per square yard constitutes a stony soil. Dries out rather quickly.

Preparation of different soils

CHALK   In autumn or winter shallow dig the plot adding plenty of well-rotted manure, compost or peat. This will build up the soil and create water-holding properties. Dig when soil is moist but not sticky. Apply roughly 4 lbs. compost to every square yard. Leave the soil to settle at least three weeks before planting.

CLAY OR HEAVY LOAM   Artificial drainage is sometimes the only way to cope with the water-logged soil. Where the drainage is very poor make a small soak-away. Dig a hole 2 ft. wide and 2 ft. deep at the lowest point in your garden. Fill the hole with stones or broken bricks to a depth of one foot. Fill up with top soil to level off with the garden. To promote surface drainage add coarse sand to the top soil. In early autumn when the land will be easier to work, dig over the ground with a fork and leave rough. To lighten the soil add compost, leaf mould or peat moss – 56 lbs. to 1 cwt. spread over 10 sq. yds. Leave the soil for the winter frost to break down the lumps. In February complete the breaking down process with a top dressing of lime – $\frac{3}{4}$ lb. per sq. yd. A month later, on a dry day, rake over the ground when the clods of earth should break down into a tilth.

It may need several rakings. This heavy soil warms up very slowly after the winter so planting must be done later.

Spread lime on top of the soil immediately after the autumn digging if you did not add manure.

PEAT   To make a peaty soil really fertile make sure there is good drainage – artificial if necessary. In the autumn after digging spread lime generously on top – 1 lb. per sq. yd. When digging incorporate some top soil if available.

SANDY   Do not dig more than 6 ins. deep. To bind the soil and make it heavier lay strips of unrotted straw in each trench as you dig. Add 60–100 lbs. of compost to every 10 sq. yds. Turves or heavy soil can also be incorporated. Add lime two or three months later at the rate of ½ lb. per sq. yd. Lime has a binding effect but it is too often 'leached out' – rain washing it through into the subsoil – unless there is plenty of coarse material in the top soil to hold it there.

STONY   Rain tends to wash the plant foods through the soil. To counteract this, shallow dig and add the well-rotted manure or compost just below the surface. Apply 100 lbs. to 10 sq. yds.

LOAM   Dig the ground in the autumn and add a light dressing of compost.

Digging improves your soil by breaking it down and letting the air into the lower soil. It helps to quicken the decomposition of the humus and the ground becomes warmer for earlier sowing.

Lime

Each type of soil is either acid, alkaline or neutral depending upon the amount of lime it contains. Peat with no lime in it is an acid soil whilst chalk is an alkaline soil.

If you are in doubt about the nature of your soil, buy a soil test kit available from the larger garden centres or shops. They are not expensive. The result will show whether your soil is acid or alkaline. It will indicate how much lime (or peat) your soil needs to make good the deficiencies and to ensure successful growing.

Hydrated lime is the easiest to use. It is a good soil conditioner and important in a herb garden, where most herbs prefer a neutral or alkaline soil. Lime is a natural plant food and breaks down the humus by releasing other elements necessary for sturdy plant growth. Lime helps to break down heavy soils and to bind sandy soil. It is helpful in keeping plants pest free.

For all its goodness it must be emphasised that too much lime can cause plant leaves to turn yellow. Usually lime is added after the autumn digging. It is spread evenly over the soil and the rain washes it into the ground.

Lime should never be added at the same time as other top dressings otherwise valuable plant foods are lost.

In a herb garden lime should be applied to the soil every second or third year either in the autumn or spring.

Compost

To cultivate intensively and produce healthy vigorous herb plants, there needs to be plenty of humus in the soil on which the plants can feed.

Humus is rotted down organic matter present in the soil. It must constantly be built up to replace the goodness which has been taken out by the plants or washed out by the rain.

Bulky organic matter is added to increase the number of bacteria in the soil and so improve the texture.

Well-rotted manure is not easy to obtain and in a small garden often difficult to store. The answer is to use vegetable compost. Whether you make your own or prefer to buy ready bagged compost is your choice, but it is easy to make and takes up very little space in the garden.

To keep the compost heap within bounds surround a small area with wire netting, staked at the corners, or use wooden planks. An area $2\frac{1}{2}$ ft. square and $2\frac{1}{2}$ ft. high should be sufficient. Alternatively a small wooden or PVC bottomless bin can be bought. These have removable boards at one side so you can easily get at the rotted down compost at the base.

Choose a sheltered corner of the garden and remove a few inches of the top soil – keep this to one side. Place the wire, planks or bin on top. Put a layer of twigs on the bottom for drainage and to aerate the compost. On to this tip your garden refuse. Use leaves (but not ever-greens), weeds well mixed with lawn mowings, straw or old hay and wood ash from the bonfire. Add the roots and leaves of comfrey. These help to break down the compost. Put kitchen waste on the heap, but use only vegetable matter; fruit and vegetable peelings, egg shells, coffee grounds and tea leaves – even tea bags! Any herb refuse can also be added from the soft stemmed herbs.

Built up the bin in layers of about 6 ins., alternating the refuse with a one inch layer of soil. Use the top soil you dug away from the bottom of the bin for this. Then add another layer of refuse and a sprinkling of lime. And so on to fill up the bin. Always keep the top of the heap flat and packed down tightly. Cover with an old sack after each addition so the heat will build up and lead to faster decomposition. The cover should also keep out the rain.

When the bin is full make about four or five holes in the heap with a stick to allow the heap to breathe. For faster results you can then add an activator such as old manure. After 8–10 weeks the compost should be ready to use. You may prefer to buy your compost. It is better for herb growing to choose an organic preparation sold by a reliable supplier.

Annual herbs such as dill, basil, chervil, sweet marjoram, parsley and summer savory are grown from seed. The seed is sown indoors in February or March and out-of-doors from April onwards, when danger from frost is over. Many perennial plants can also be grown successfully from seed.

You will need your plants early in the year so if possible start them indoors – whether it is greenhouse, garden frame or in the house.

Use clean seed boxes or clay flower-pots. Put pieces of broken brick in the bottom of the flower pots for the drainage. Use a good seed compost. To make your own, mix together in equal parts coarse sand, peat moss and garden loam. Sift milled sphagnum moss over the top of the seed bed after tamping the soil down.

Fill the containers to $\frac{1}{2}$ or $\frac{3}{4}$ of an inch from the top. Firm the soil down using a block of wood which just fits the size of your box, and in the flower pots use your fingertips. About 8 lbs. compost fills a seed box $14\frac{1}{2}$ ins. $\times$ 9 ins., and about 3 lbs. compost fills a seed box $8\frac{3}{4}$ ins. $\times$ $6\frac{1}{2}$ ins. Moisten the compost and leave the boxes for twenty-four hours to warm up the soil.

Sow the seeds thinly pressing fine seeds, such as summer savory, into the soil. Cover the larger seeds with more sifted sphagnum. Cover the containers with a sheet of glass, then newspaper or brown paper. Keep them in an even temperature of about 60°F. Once the seeds have begun to grow the paper and glass can be removed and the containers brought into the light. Do not stand them in direct sunlight. Remember always to keep the soil moist, either by standing the containers in water for a while or by a fine mist spray on top.

Once the seedlings have 2 sets of leaves they should be pricked out into other seed boxes filled with finely sieved, rich organic potting compost, about 2 ins. apart. Finally the seedlings must be hardened off before being planted into their final position out of doors. This can be done by moving the boxes or pots into the coolest part of the house or into a cold frame with the cover removed.

In later months and to have a succession of plants sow similar annual seeds out of doors. Sow on a warm moist day. Rake the top soil until it is a fine tilth. Seeds can be sown in shallow drills in rows, or scattered on the surface if you prefer them growing in a clump. They are covered with soil to a depth equal to twice their own diameter and the fine seeds should be mixed with sand so that they come up evenly. When sown in drills rake the soil lightly over the top of the seeds and firm down the earth with the back of the rake.

Germination time for annuals is usually about 12 to 14 days and for perennials about 3 to 4 weeks. When the seedlings have 2 sets of leaves they can be carefully thinned out to their appropriate distance apart. If the thinnings are good enough you can try planting them in another patch in the garden, or you can dry them. Even these small leaves should be full of flavour.

There are some perennial herbs, such as french tarragon or the mints, which cannot be grown from seed. These must be purchased as plants in pots from a herb nursery. You can obtain most of the perennials in this way and save a great deal of time. Planting perennial herbs from pots needs care if the plants are not to suffer too much of a setback. Container grown plants can be put into the garden at any time of the year except during frost or snow, provided the weather is warm and moist. You must be prepared to keep the plant well watered in dry conditions.

Water the herb in the pot and plant out on a day when the soil is moist but not too wet. Carefully remove the plant from the pot – a firm tap on the side of the pot will loosen a reluctant plant. If the plants are small do not disturb the root ball, but gently loosen any outside coiled-up roots. Dig the hole with a trowel and plant firmly with the top of the soil ball just below ground level. Fill loose soil round the soil ball and firm it down with the handle of the trowel.

When planting out the shrubby herbs such as rosemary or bay, set them in to the depth of the 'soil mark' showing on the stems. The hole should be wide enough to allow their roots to be spread out. Put some peat or leaf mould in the bottom of the hole before putting in the herb. Water all herbs in well after planting.

Propagating

There are several methods by which you can increase your stock of perennials. Throughout the growing season you can take stem and root cuttings as well as layering plants. Root division can take place in the autumn or spring. Stem cuttings or 'slips' can be taken from a well-established herb plant at any time in the spring or summer. Mint is one of the easiest herbs to increase in this way, so are rosemary, lemon balm and sage.

Take firm strong stems 4–6 ins. long with plenty of leaves on and cut them just below a leaf bud. Remove leaves from the lower half of the stem. Dip the ends into water and then into a hormone rooting powder. Fill a flower pot (remember the drainage) with a leafmold compost for cuttings or some organic seed and cutting compost, to within ½ in. of the top. Firm it lightly and, using a pencil as a dibber, put the cuttings round the rim of the pot to a depth of one third of their length. Firm the compost round the base of the cuttings. Keep the soil moist. Leave the pot in the shade until the cuttings show signs of growth.

Alternatively, dig a shallow trench in a shady spot in the garden. Run some sand along the bottom of the trench, dip the cuttings in hormone powder and plant them out. Firm the soil well and keep it moist. Many plants when growing vigorously send up new stems from their roots. These include rosemary, sage, lemon verbena, tarragon and thyme.

To take root cuttings choose those roots which are $\frac{1}{8}$–$\frac{1}{4}$ in. thick and cut them into pieces 2 ins. long. Fill a seed box with a loam or sand, peat moss and loam to within 1 in. of the top. Lay the cuttings on the soil about 2 ins. apart and cover with $\frac{1}{2}$ in. of soil. Water well then cover the box with a sheet of glass and newspaper. Leave the box in the shade. When new growth appears transplant into individual pots for putting into the ground at a later date. Layering is by far the easiest way of increasing your stock of perennial herbs. Some plants layer themselves – the mints especially.

Choose a strong branch which is already growing close to the ground. At a point about 10–12 ins. from the tip bend the stem and make a small slanting cut. Dip the cut in hormone rooting powder. Bury the actual bend of the stem in a small hole dug beneath it and filled with compost. Secure the bend firmly in the ground with a piece of bent wire or a large hairpin, and stake the remainder of the branch in an upright position. Roots usually take about 6 weeks to form. Finally cut the rooted stem from the parent plant and plant it elsewhere.

Through the years plants such as chives, tarragon, sorrel and costmary increase enormously in size. By lifting and dividing them in spring or autumn you can multiply your stock. Dig up the herb and either pull or cut the root clump apart. Replant the divided roots into containers or into the garden and keep well watered until they are established.

Management

Whether you are going to sell cut fresh herbs, dried herbs or plants in pots, you need to get a high yield from your herb bed. Good management is therefore essential throughout the growing season. At all times keep the plot free of weeds. Cultivate the surface by hoeing to a depth of 2 or 3 ins. to break up the soil. This lets in the air and stops the surface from caking in dry weather. It also helps to keep the weeds down.

Some herbs need a moist position in the garden and these, angelica, parsley and mint, should be kept watered during a dry spell. Put a label in the ground by those perennial plants which die down in winter, so you will not forget where they are.

In spring or autumn spread fertiliser over the ground between the plants and lightly fork it in. Fertilisers are concentrated plant foods which should be added regularly to soils. A good organic fertiliser is old manure. Alternatively spread peat over the soil. This helps to keep the weeds down and the moisture in the soil. At the end of the growing season after flowering, cut back half the years's growth of your shrubby perennial herbs. This will encourage bushy growth during the next season. You can use the leaves and flowers for drying.

PATIO PLANTS AND WINDOW BOXES

Preparation

Growing herbs for profit on a patio needs fairly intensive cultivation methods. If your patio is large enough you can grow the herbs for sale in pots. Otherwise it is perhaps easier to sell them as cut fresh herbs or dried herbs. Plants on the patio growing as they do in a confined space – a container, a wall box or a window box, a raised bed or a hanging basket – need to have a slightly richer soil than those herbs in the garden.

There are many different types of container available, tubs, clay pots, strawberry jars, wire hanging baskets, wooden troughs and window boxes and other pots or boxes in which herbs can look most attractive. When choosing containers for herbs make sure they meet the following basic requirements:

(1) Adequate drainage. Hole in the bottom to allow water to get away.

(2) Adequate depth – not less than 9 ins.

(3) Adequate strength. Remember quite a lot of soil

is needed to fill a comparatively small box and soil is heavy.

Always stand your containers, whether plastic or wooden, on the bricks to ensure good circulation of air. Make sure the drained water can get away and so avoid a wooden container becoming rotten.

Window-sill boxes should also have good drainage. A layer of gravel in the bottom of the box provides this where there are no drainage holes. You can keep herbs in pots on an outside window-sill provided they stand on a layer of gravel either in the window box or on a tray. Make sure both tray and pots are secure on the sill.

In a raised bed on a patio drainage holes – short lengths of pipe – must be placed at intervals round the base of the wall.

Whether you are re-using old containers or have bought new ones, they should all be well washed in a solution of washing soda before being filled. For the raised bed or other containers, cover the base with a layer of broken 'crocks' then a layer of gravel. Fill with a good potting compost, such as Pro-Mix. This might seem rather an expensive outlay for the raised circular bed, but it will last for several years, especially if there is regular feeding of the soil. If sowing seeds in the container fill it with compost to within one inch of the top. If planting out perennials then fill so that when the herbs are planted the surface of the soil will also be about one inch from the top. Firm the compost down and water it well. Leave for 24 hours before sowing.

Planting

From April onwards seeds of annual herbs can be sown directly into the containers. Sow seeds sparing on top of the soil, firm down and sprinkle a further layer of soil on top. Water again by mist spraying. When the seedlings reach the four-leaf stage they should be thinned out to the correct distance apart. Alternatively, annual herb plants can be purchased from a herb nursery from May onwards.

Perennial herbs can be purchased from the nursery at any time of the year, provided there is no snow or frost, except for those which die down in winter. The plants need a good soaking before being put in their final growing position. Remove the plant from the pot taking care not to disturb the root ball. Make a big enough hole in the container to take the roots adequately and put in the plant. Fill up with soil and firm the plant down. It must be set in firmly enough so that when you give the plant a slight tug it will not come out of the soil. Water the plant well but not fiercely. Use a sprinkler nozzle on the watering can. Be careful not to overfill your containers, the herbs must have adequate space to spread.

When the containers have been filled with plants, shade them from direct sunlight until they have recovered from the move – two or three days. Remember that hot sun and drying winds act on the exposed sides of the containers in which the herbs are growing. Where possible place your patio plants so they will be in the shade during the hottest part of the day.

Propagation

Where space permits you can easily increase your stock of herbs by taking cuttings using a propagating box. Take a wooden box about 12 ins. deep and make a few drainage holes in the bottom. Put a layer of broken 'crocks' on the bottom then a layer of peat. Half fill the box with moist John Innes rooting compost. Take cuttings 3–6 ins. long from strong growing tip of the perennial herbs in spring or autumn. Remove leaves from the lower half of the cutting, dip the end in water then in hormone rooting powder. Firmly plant each cutting to one third of its depth in your box. Spray with water. Cover the box with a sheet of glass and stand it in the shade. In very hot weather spray the cuttings with water, they will take root much more quickly. The cuttings will have rooted once new leaves appear. Transplant your rooted cuttings carefully so as not to disturb the soil round the roots.

Other herbs can be increased by dividing the roots in the autumn. Lift the plant and separate the roots by gently pulling them apart or, with a spade, sever them neatly downwards.

Management

Container grown plants need much more water than those grown in the garden. Every other day check the soil and never allow it to dry out completely. If the soil just beneath the surface is dry the plant needs watering. Water from the top with a sprinkler nozzle on the watering can.

If the container can be moved, place it in a dish of water and let the soil absorb water at its own pace. When the surface soil is moist the plant has had enough – it could take at least an hour. A good tip for deciding when a clay flower pot needs watering, is gently to tap the side of the pot. If a hollow ring is heard the plant needs water, if a dull thud then there is already sufficient moisture.

Window boxes or pots will need watering every day in warm weather, especially if they are in a sunny position where there is rapid evaporation of water. Containers should be kept free of weeds at all times.

Regular feeding during the growing season with an organic liquid fertiliser should be maintained. Use Maxicrop, an organic seaweed plant food, every 10–14 days. Proportions are usually 3 teaspoons Maxicrop to one gallon of water. Pull off any yellowing leaves.

INDOOR HERBS

Preparation

Most herbs which can be successfully grown in containers out of doors, can also be grown indoors. For indoor growing it is most likely you will be buying your plants direct from a nursery.

When buying herbs look for:

(1) Small stocky plants.

(2) Fibrous root formation coming through the base of the pot. This is good and denotes a well-established plant.

You can buy most perennial herbs at any time of the year and, provided they are not too large, they will grow well indoors.

Annual herb plants you can buy from May onwards. In the autumn sow seeds in pots or boxes. From all these plants you can have fresh sprigs to sell throughout the winter.

When preparing to grow herbs indoors the following basic requirements are important:

(1) Adequate drainage of pots, boxes or other containers.

(2) Adequate light is essential for good plant growth. A sunny window sill is best but is not absolutely necessary.

(3) Adequate warmth. Herbs like an even temperature of around 60–70°F rather than extremes of hot or cold.

(4) Adequate ventilation or air. No stuffy rooms. Windows can be opened a crack for air provided there are no draughts.

(5) Adequate humidity. The most common reason for failure is a hot dry atmosphere. If in doubt about the level of humidity place a dish full of water near the growing herbs. The water will evaporate and keep the air damp around the plants.

Make as much use as possible of your available space in the flat or house. Try and have herbs at all stages of growth. Have more than one plant of a herb at the same stage so that cutting can be done in rotation. Constant cutting of one plant will weaken it beyond recall.

Scrub new or used pots, boxes or containers in a weak solution of washing soda. Put a layer of broken 'crocks' in the bottom then a layer of gravel. Where your container has no drainage holes put in a good thick layer of gravel. Fill the containers to within one inch of the rim with sand, peat moss and loam or any organic seed and cutting compost. Firm it down and water well. Leave it for 24 hours to settle.

Planting

Sow annual seeds thinly in the containers during the autumn or spring. Cover the seeds with a further thin layer of soil unless the seeds are very fine when they can just be pressed into the soil. Firm the soil. Water and place a sheet of glass then newspaper on top. Once the seeds have germinated remove the glass and paper and gradually bring the containers into full light. When the seedlings have reached the four leaf stage they should be thinned to the correct number of plants per pot. Not more than six plants in an 8-in. pot.

To help the plants become established more quickly, cover the pot with a polythene bag and secure it with a rubber band. Make sure the polythene does not touch the plants.

For perennial plants soak them well before transplanting. Have a container sufficiently large enough for their roots. Firm down well and water.

Where the pots or containers have drainage holes stand them on trays or boxes on a layer of shingle. This will absorb excess water and help maintain humidity.

Propagation

During the winter the constant cutting of fresh sprigs of herbs will weaken the plants. Renew the plants in spring. Follow the instructions again for sowing annual seeds. Where space permits you can take cuttings from perennial herbs in autumn or spring.

Take one or two cuttings 3–6 ins. long using only good strong growing tips from the plant. Remove the leaves from the lower half of the stem. Dip the ends in water then into hormone rooting powder. Plant them to a third of their depth round the edge of a pot filled with wet sand. Cover with a polythene bag – make sure it does not touch the cuttings – and put the pot in a warm but shady spot. When new leaves start growing your cuttings will have rooted. This may take at least a month, so do not throw them away in disgust earlier than that! However, if after a fortnight, the leaves turn yellow and the stems go black pull them out and start again.

Management

Where plants cannot be sited on a sunny window-sill try to put them in the sun for a short while each day. Move the herb pots round every other day so that all parts of the plant get the same amount of air and light. Keep the plants free from weeds.

Watering is all-important for indoor herbs. Check the soil just under the surface every day. If is is dry use water which is at room temperature. Sprinkle the leaves with water every now and again. Regular feeding with a liquid plant food should be carried out every 10–14 days during the growing period. Use fish emulsion or Maxicrop, following directions on the container. These are organically based.

IN THE GREENHOUSE

Preparation

A greenhouse can be used for intensive herb production. If it can be kept free from frost herbs can be grown throughout the year. It is not the easiest way to grow herbs, because the plants need more of everything; food, watering and ventilation. The problem of pests can get beyond control and you may become discouraged. Nevertheless with care and watchfulness you can produce good herbs to sell.

Start by using a disinfectant throughout the greenhouse. Clean with LF 10 as directed on the tin, provided the greenhouse can be well aired for several days after cleaning and before stocking with plants.

It is important the greenhouse be properly shaded during the summer, otherwise the sun will scorch your plants. Some people cover the glass with the Seran screening that has a 53 to 63 per cent stretch. Others use mesh shading cloth, of which there is a great variety, to provide shade. Whichever you use, remove it in the autumn. Scrub all pots and containers in a strong solution of washing soda. Fill greenhouse bed or containers with a good loam or potting compost such as Pro-Mix and firm down the soil. Water it well and leave for 24 hours before planting herbs or sowing seeds.

Planting

Sow your seeds in their final growing position whether it is in a pot, box or a greenhouse bed. Firm down the soil, sow the seeds and cover with a light sprinkling of more soil.

Water them in and cover pots or boxes with glass and newspaper until germination has begun. When the seedlings each have 2 pairs of leaves, thin them out to their correct distance apart. If in pots, do not have more than 4 plants in a 6-in. pot.

For purchased plants give them a good soaking before transplanting into their growing position. Make sure there is plenty of room for the roots to spread.

Propagation

For propagating follow the instructions given for indoor plants, p. 63, or use a propagating box, p. 60.

Proper ventilation is important in a greenhouse. Plants need fresh air without draughts. Unless the temperature outside is very low, a top ventilator can be opened for a few hours in the middle of each day.

Watering should be done each day during the growing season but only if the soil beneath the surface is dry. Use rain water where possible and water thoroughly. In the summer syringe the plant leaves, the greenhouse walls, glass and staging with tepid water to keep up a high humidity. In the winter keep the glass clean so that your herbs will get maximum benefit from the sun.

Keep beds and containers free of weeds. Throw away all dead or diseased plants or leaves – do not leave them lying about in the greenhouse. Always remove yellowing leaves which could indicate the presence of greenfly.

Never allow moss or lichen to grow on the pots, it stifles the plants. Remember that proper ventilation, correct watering and cleanliness in your greenhouse will ensure strong healthy herbs.

PESTS AND DISEASES

There are only a few diseases which affect herb plants. The most troublesome is the 'damping off' disease which affects seedling herbs, especially when they are grown under glass. The base of the stems wither and become black. It is caused by over watering, sowing seeds too thickly or using unsterilised compost. Preventive measures are:

(1) Use a seed dressing, such as milled sphagnum.

(2) Be very careful not to overwater; the sowing medium should not be dry, but not wet, either. Avoid soaking the foliage when spraying in summer; if the plant looks sprightly, it probably doesn't need misting.

Be sure that the drainage is adequate and that the seedlings do not stand in water. Don't delay thinning seedlings – overcrowding invites trouble.

(3) Remove and burn those seedlings already affected by the disease.

Where mint is subjected to frequent changes of temperature, there is a danger it will be attacked by rust. This is a fungus disease. The rust spores appear on the underneath of the leaves and gradually spread up the stems of the plant. The only remedy is to cut the mint down and burn it. If the soil in which the mint has been growing has been steam-sterilized, the spores do not appear.

The pest most likely to attack your herb plants is the greenfly. These appear in clusters on the undersides of leaves and on young shoots during the spring and summer. The leaves curl up and the plant becomes weak. To treat greenfly spray the plants regularly with soapy water using pure soap. A solution of green soft soap is most effective.

Another annoying pest is the red spider mite. It is very small and moves very fast. It weaves a white web on the underside of the leaves on which it feeds. The leaves become hard and snap easily. The red spider mite appears most often in hot, dry conditions. Greenhouse plants are particularly susceptible. Preventive treatment is to keep the atmosphere in the greenhouse humid by frequently spraying the walls, glass, path and staging with water.

Once the red spider mite has appeared carefully spray the plants with a weak solution of yellow naphtha soap and water.

The more care you take in looking after and producing sturdy herb plants the less likely they are to succumb to the onslaught of pests and diseases.

5

Harvesting, Drying
and Storing

HARVESTING

Traditional harvest time is in the autumn when an entire
crop is gathered in for storing and selling throughout the
winter. Gathering herbs can go on the whole year round
depending on where they are grown and whether you
plan to sell pot plants, freshly cut sprigs or dried herbs. If
you have space and time for all three methods then your
selling programme can be a continuous one.

POT-GROWN HERBS

Annual herbs in pots will necessarily have only a limited
period of sale. If you can start them early in the year
under glass and with heat, the period can be lengthened.
Usually annuals in pots can be sold from the end of May
onwards. Much time and work is needed for annuals. The
herbs are sown in boxes and pricked out at the four leaf
stage into potting compost in small soft black polythene
pots, which are sold for the purpose. These must be kept
free of weeds and well watered and the plant must not be
allowed to get leggy.

Perennial herbs in pots can be sold all the year round.
You can have a succession of plants at different stages of

growth so you do not have to sell all the plants at the same time. Some can be grown in the greenhouse, others out of doors.

The evergreen perennials are the herbs to grow for the winter. These are rosemary, lavender, bay, hyssop, winter savory, thyme and welsh onion. It is easier to have as many herbs as possible growing in their pots in the ground. You lift them as they are required. When the plants get big, lift them to see if roots are growing through the bottom of the pots into the ground. Re-pot them if necessary into more potting compost in larger pots. Keep the pots free of weeds and well watered.

FRESH CUT HERB SPRIGS

Bunches of herbs sold in greengrocer's shops are a familiar sight. This is therefore one of the easiest ways to sell your herbs. You will need a good number of herb plants to market them in this manner as each plant will need time to recover after cutting. As soon as your herbs are bushy or large enough they are ready for harvesting.

Cut sprigs 6–8 ins. long from the end of each stem. This will encourage side shoots and bushy growth, and will provide you at a later date, with many more sprigs to cut.

DRIED HERBS

Leaves

The flavour, colour and scent of the dried herb depends upon the amount of volatile oil present in the leaves at the time of cutting. The volatile oil content is at its highest just before the plant begins to flower.

To ensure that the oil is not wasted in the production of flower heads the buds should always be removed as soon as they appear. This is also the best time to cut and dry the first crop of leafy stems. Afterwards the harvesting can continue throughout the growing season provided the plant is well established and the cutting does not weaken it. The following exceptions should be noted:

(1) Russian tarragon should be cut when young, at about 2–2½ ft. tall. Otherwise the leaves may be bitter. Test a leaf before launching into a drying programme.

(2) French tarragon should be cut when it is about 8–12 ins, high.

(3) The broad-leaved or common sage, which does not flower, can be cut over a long period from early spring to late autumn.

(4) Rosemary, summer savory and thyme should be cut when the plants are in full flower.

(5) Bay can be cut the whole year round.

(6) Leave some dill and fennel plants to go to seed for harvesting in the autumn.

(7) The leaves of the following herbs are not dried. Borage, chamomile, cornflower – the flowers are dried. Marigold – the petals are dried.

Anise, caraway, coriander – the seeds are harvested.

Garlic – the bulbs are lifted when the leaves are dead.

During the growing season perennial herbs for drying can be cut back to about a third of their growth at each cutting. Afterwards the herbs will need time to recover. Make sure you have enough plants of each herb so that your selling programme can continue throughout the summer.

In the autumn cut the shrubby perennials back to half their year's growth. Leave bay alone, unless it is large and untidy. Other perennials die right down in winter. Annual herbs can be cut to within about 4–5 ins. from the ground at each cutting during the season. They will soon grow again. You should be able to get several cuttings from your herbs.

In the autumn cut the annuals down to ground level and remove the plant. Ideally herbs should be gathered in the morning when they are quite dry, after the dew has dried off but before the sun has affected the volatile oils.

Try not to gather your herbs when they are wet, they

lose flavour and are much more difficult to handle. Beware too of heavy rain, hail and high winds all of which will bruise and damage the tender leaves. The herbs should be left to recover. Cut the herbs cleanly with scissors, a sharp knife or secateurs. Do not harvest more leaves than you can easily cope with at any one time. Speed is vital when drying in order to retain both colour and flavour. Handle the herbs with care to avoid any bruising of the leaves.

Immediately after cutting, gently but quickly wash the herbs in tepid water – not ice-cold water straight from the tap. Shake off the excess water and start the drying process. Container-grown perennial herbs must be cut with care, do not take too many leaves off a plant at a time. Otherwise the herb will try and compensate for its lack of leaves by sending down deep roots.

During the growing months the annuals can be cut to within 4 ins. of the pot at each cutting. In the autumn cut the plant right down and remove it. Indoor and greenhouse herbs can be cut judiciously all the year round.

Flowers and petals

Flowers for drying must be collected when they are fully open and not wilted or discoloured in any way. You may find as a result that you will be gathering them in ones and twos. Make sure they are quite dry when you pick them. Handle them gently and do not pile them on top of one another. Flower heads are never washed. Lavender flowers are harvested just as they come into full bloom. Cut them with long stems. Gather petals of scented roses when absolutely dry and use only the best unblemished ones. After cutting the marigold flowers, carefully pull away the petals as they have to be well spread out to dry.

Seed

Anise, caraway, coriander, dill and fennel seed are all ready to harvest when the seed capsules turn brown.

Choose a warm dry day and cut off the whole seed-head halfway down the stem.

Drying

The process of drying is simply to extract the water content of the herb. In carrying out this process care must be taken so that the volatile oil contained in the herb is not lost. Your aim is to produce dried herbs which are green and taste like fresh herbs when liquid is added.

The important points to remember are:

(1) the whole process should be completed as carefully and as quickly as possible. Cut, wash if necessary, dry and store. The exceptions to this rule are thick fleshy leaves, flowers petals and seeds. These are all dried slowly.

(2) there must be adequate ventilation and a good circulation of air round the herbs to carry off the evaporating moisture.

(3) the temperature must be right for each herb. Extremes of heat will cause the herbs to go brown and lose flavour.

(4) herbs should be dried in the dark. Light affects the volatile oil content.

The most successful drying method is one which will fulfill all the requirements for good dried herbs.

Place the herbs on racks or special drying trays in a cool oven (not above 100°F), a plate-warming oven, the airing cupboard or in the vicinity of the boiler. You can use a warm darkened room or even your garden shed, in warm weather, for slow drying some of the herbs. Unless you are drying bay leaves, do not take the leaves off the stems.

Some herbs such as thyme and summer savory can have the dried stems mixed with the leaves. Chives and welsh onion are chopped small before drying and they are always dried on their own. For drying herbs in small quantities you can put them straight on to a piece of muslin cut to fit one of the racks or shelves in the oven. The draw-back with this method is that the muslin is not taut and the herbs, when they are dry, stick to it.

Drying herbs on a larger scale makes it worthwhile constructing some drying trays. They are easy and inexpensive to make, and can be of any size to suit your needs. A convenient size would be one slightly smaller than an oven shelf. Using pieces of battening wood $\frac{3}{4}$ in. $\times$ $1\frac{1}{2}$ in. make up a sturdy frame. Over this stretch a piece of stiff nylon net and secure it to the frame with staples.

Spread the herbs out evenly on your trays. Do not pile them and do not dry two different herbs on one tray. Keep one tray especially for drying chives and welsh onion, otherwise their strong flavours will spoil that of the more delicate herbs.

Put the trays in the oven in lowest heat possible, and never more than 100°F. Leave the door slightly ajar. Where two or three trays are in the oven at the same time, change over the upper and lower one after a time to ensure that the herbs will be evenly dried.

When drying herbs in a plate-warming oven, near a boiler or in a warm dark room, support the corners of the tray with small blocks of wood (four cotton reels will do) so that the air can circulate. If the boiler is not in a cupboard cover the drying tray with paper to keep out the light and keep off flies and dust. If you are drying a number of different herbs at the same time it is advisable to make a note of the names. Stick labels on each tray. Herbs are not always easy to identify after drying.

To dry flowers and marigold petals use the trays and put them in a warm dark cupboard, but where the air can circulate. Dry rose petals on trays in a darkened airy room covering the petals with a piece of muslin. It may take at least a week for them to become completely dry.

Seeds must be absolutely dry before you can store them. After cutting the seed heads, tie all the stems together in a bunch and hang them upside down with the seed-heads in a large paper bag. When all the seeds have fallen from the capsules into the paper bag, spread them evenly over the trays. Leave in the garden shed or airy room covered with thick paper for 10–14 days.

How to know when your herbs are dry

LEAVES   They should be crisp and crackle to the touch. Stems should snap easily if being mixed with the leaves; otherwise they need not be fully dry.

FLOWERS AND PETALS   They should be crisp with no trace of stickiness.

SEEDS   They must be hard and difficult to break between finger and thumb nail. If they smell at all musty, they are not yet completely dry.

When the herbs are fully dried remove them from the warmth and allow to cool.

Leaves can be rubbed off the stems by hand, unless you prefer to leave them whole. Alternatively you can rub the leaves through a coarse sieve. Flowers and petals are all left whole. Seeds should also be left whole, the flavour is quickly lost if they are ground to a powder, but put them through a fine sieve to remove dust and unwanted matter.

Storing

Once dried, the herbs need to be kept airtight and in the dark. Provided these basic requirements are fulfilled the quality of your dried herbs will be maintained. The best containers are coloured or opaque glass jars with screw tops.

Avoid the use of storage tins unless you put the herbs in cotton bags within the tin. The metal may alter the flavour of the herb over a period of time if it is in contact the herb. Never store different herbs together in one jar. Carefully label each herb jar and add the date. From your store of dried herbs you can put one or two spoonfuls into attractive pots, jars or small polythene bags for sale at any time. Do not keep dried herbs for longer than 10–12 months. The flavour, scent and colour will gradually deteriorate.

You will find that only a few plants will produce a surprisingly large amount of dried herb. Where growing space is limited it might therefore be advisable to sell dried rather than fresh herbs.

6

Marketing and Outlets

Marketing

Presentation is of prime importance when selling your
herbs. Care and consideration should go into making
them look as attractive as possible. No one will consider
buying your herbs if they are not at their best. Make sure
your pot-grown herbs are sturdy, vigorous plants with
plenty of good coloured foliage. Each plant should be
compact and well-shaped, the whole effect pleasing the eye
and building up your reputation. Label the herbs clearly.

Fresh herbs should be cut on the morning of sale. Select
sprigs with good foliage of equal length. Tie the individual herbs in small bunches of the same size and trim
level. You could bunch together sprigs of thyme, parsley
and a bay leaf – all ready for the cooking pot.

Whilst awaiting sale the bunches can sometimes be put
into jars of water. In which case no sort of wrapping is
needed. Alternatively you can place the sprigs in polythene bags and secure with a wire twist. Make sure the
labels can be easily seen. You can sell your culinary dried
herbs in little glass jars or polythene, cotton and muslin
bags tied securely with thin string or colourful cotton.
Keep them of uniform size and write the name of the
herb where it can be seen. You might add to it a sugges-
tion for using the herb.

Seeds can be packed and sold in the same manner, one or two spoonfuls in each. Secure the bags and label them clearly. Alternatively use little plastic pots.

When you sell seeds you must make it clear to the customer that they are for household or culinary use only. In England, there are strict rules on the sale of garden seeds. If you put less than an ounce (25g.) of dried herb or seed in each container, the weight need not be marked. This is important since there are statutory regulations regarding weights and measures which you must observe when selling your produce in amounts over 1 oz. (25g.).

There are many other ways in which you can use your dried herbs to make saleable products. Lavender bags, pot-pourris, herb cushions, herb sachets, bath pochettes, herb teas and sweet herb posies are simple to make and can look most attractive. Using herbs in this way will widen your sales outlets and so attract other groups of customers.

As a producer of herbs on a small scale your sales outlets are necessarily somewhat limited. It is unlikely you will be able to offer a continuous supply in sufficient quantity to make it worthwhile going to wholesale markets or to join a producer co-operative. But you do have advantages not always available to a large supplier. They lie in the quality and freshness of your products and in the personal contact you will have with your buyer. You must make the most of these assets when setting forth to market your herbs. Depending upon whereabouts in the country you live, the following suggestions may provide you with possible markets.

Local shops

Spend time in visiting those shops which you think would be interested in selling herbs. Try the greengrocer, the delicatessen, the florist, perhaps the grocer. Any one of these may buy your herbs from you outright, or sell them for you and take a commission. Discovering which herbs will sell most readily may be a matter of trial and error. The familiar herbs, parsley, sage, thyme and mint will always have a sale. You may prefer to grow these on a fairly steady basis whilst experimenting with some of the unusual herbs which will, until they become known, be more difficult to sell.

You could supply the family butcher with parsley and sage, and the fishmonger with dill or fennel. A small café or teashop might be keen to buy herbs either for garnish or use in cooking and baking.

For marketing your dried herbs and those products which you may make by utilising them, visit the small specialist shops, the gift shop or boutique. Many shops like to sell 'locally grown' produce. The label stands for freshness and the customer is willing to pay a little more for it. You could try and offer a small regular supply of just one or two herbs which are in constant demand.

Roadside stands

A good outlet for your herbs and the best if you have other products to sell alongside. It is easiest if you live in a country area where customers can stop and park a car without difficulty. This method of selling has advantages over others since the customer comes direct to you and there are no commission charges with which to cope.

Before you set up a board at your garden gate, you should check with your local authority that you are not contravening any bye-laws. Set up a small stall when you have plenty to sell. Unless customers are actually walking past your gate, it is unlikely they will stop for a few handfuls of herbs. Have prices clearly marked where they can easily be seen. Keep the prices to round figures of one or two coins if possible. Do not lurk about your stall – either stand or sit nearby ready to offer help, or get on with another job in the garden. Display your board in a prominent position and direct your customers to where they may see and buy your produce.

Wholefood and health shops

These are good outlets for herbs provided (*a*) you have a sufficient quantity to maintain supplies and (*b*) you declare that your herbs are completely organically grown. No chemical fertilisers, weed-killers or pesticides whatsoever are to be used in the production of the herbs. With the present day emphasis on the dangers of using chemicals, organically grown produce is finding a wider market.

Market Stalls

Quite a good outlet if the stall is in a busy market-place. You need to be certain of a good turnover to make the expense worthwhile. It is therefore impractical for the small producer to hire an entire stall once a week, and impossible for a daily market. It might be possible to make arrangements with an established stall-holder. You pay something towards the hiring of the stall in return for some selling space.

Street markets come within the jurisdiction of the local authorities. You may find that a license to sell is required. For details of this and on hiring a market stall you should visit your Council offices. At the same time you should also seek advice on any bye-laws or other regulations which may apply.

Herb Suppliers

Here is a partial list of sources for plants and seeds for herb growers. All have catalogs, and will refer other sources if they are unable to fill your order. *The Herb Grower*, a magazine published quarterly, is an excellent source of information. It is published in Falls Village, Connecticut, 06031.

Caprilands Herb Farm
Silver Street
Coventry, Connecticut 06238

Casa Yerba
Box 176
Tustin, California 92680

Chientan and Company
1001 South Alvarado Street
Los Angeles, California 9006

Culpeper Ltd.
21 Bruton Street
London W1X 7DA
Mail Order: Hadstock Road
Cambridge, England

Ferndale Nursery
Akov, Minnesota 55704

Gardens of the Blue Ridge
Ashford, North Carolina 28603

The Herb Farm
Barnard Road
Granville, Massachusetts 01034

Horticulture House
347 E. 55 Street
New York, New York 10022

Indiana Botanic Gardens
626 Seventeenth Street
Hammond, Indiana 46325

Logee's Greenhouses
Danielson, Connecticut 06239

Meadowbrook Herb Garden
Wyoming, Rhode Island 02898

Merry Gardens
Camden, Maine 04843

Nichols Garden Nursery
1190 North Pacific Highway
Albany, Oregon 97321

Sunnybrook Farms Nursery
9448 Mayfield Road
Cherterland, Ohio 44026

The Tool Shed Herb Farm
Salem Center
Purdy's Station, New York 10578

Especially seeds

W. Atlee Burpee Company
P.O. Box 748
Riverside, California
      or
P.O. Box 6929
Philadelphia, Pennsylvania 19132

Greene Herb Gardens
Greene, Rhode Island 02898

Gurney Seed and Nursery
Yankton, South Dakota 57078

Shirley Morgan
Mail Box Seeds
2042 Encinal Avenue
Alameda, California 94501

George Park Seed Company, Inc.
Greenwood, South Carolina 29646

Wide World of Herbs, Ltd.
11 St. Catherine Street East
Montreal, 129 Canada

Recommended Reading

Clarkson, Rosetta. *Herbs: Their Culture and Uses.* Macmillan, 1961.

Coon, Nelson. *Using Plants for Healing.* Hearthside, 1963.

Culpeper, Nicholas. *Complete Herbal.* Wehman, 1960.

Foster, Catharine Osgood. *The Organic Gardener.* Vintage, 1972.

Freeman, Margaret. *Herbs for the Medieval Household for Cooking, Healing and Divers Uses.* Metropolitan Museum of Art, 1943.

Gregg, Richard. *Companion Plants and Herbs.* Bio Dynamic Farming and Gardening Association.

Harris, Ben. *The Compleat Herbal.* Larchmont Books, 1972.

Levy, Juliette de Bairacli Levy. *Herbal Handbook for Everyone.* Faber, 1966.

Leyel, Mrs. C. F. *The Magic of Herbs.* Harcourt, 1926.

Loewenfeld, Claire and Back, Philippa. *The Complete Book of Herbs and Spices.* Putnam, 1974.

Lucas, Richard. *Common and-Uncommon Uses of Herbs for Healthful Living.* Parker, 1969.

MacLeod, Dawn. *A Book of Herbs.* Duckworth, 1968.

McDonald, Elvin. *How to Grow Vegetables and Herbs from Seeds.* Mason/Charter, 1977.

Medsger, Oliver Perry. *Edible Wild Plants.* Macmillan, 1972.

Morton, Julia. *Herbs and Spices.* Golden, 1976.

Rutherford, Meg. *A Pattern of Herbs.* Doubleday, 1976.

Simmons, Adelma Grenier. *Herb Gardening in Five Seasons.* Hawthorn, 1964.

Webster, Helen Noyes. *Herbs – How to Grow Them and How to Use Them.* Hale, 1939.

HOW TO PREPARE A HERB TEA OR INFUSION

Whilst it is very simple to make a herb tea, there are several important points to remember. Do not use a metal pot when infusing – it may alter the flavour and effectiveness of the herb. The strength of the tea is a matter for personal taste. If you prefer a strong flavour add more leaves at the outset and infuse them for a shorter length of time.

Drink or use an infusion whilst it is fresh – either hot or chilled. If sweetening is necessary use honey rather than sugar. Infusions can be made using dried or fresh leaves and flowers.

To make one pint of herb tea:
Put 12 teaspoons chopped fresh herb (4 teaspoons dried) into a warm jug. Pour a pint of boiling water over the herb. Allow to stand 4–6 minutes. Strain and use.

For Iced Tea:
Strain the hot tea into a well chilled jug and cover it. When cool put the jug into the refrigerator for at least an hour before using.

How to Prepare a Compress

Make a strong infusion of the herb in the manner described above. Allow it to stand for about 10 minutes. Strain before using. Put pieces of cotton wool into the infusion. Lightly squeeze the cotton wool to remove the excess lotion and apply to the affected part. Use hot or cold as preferred.

7

Alphabetical List of Herbs
giving the uses of each plant

ANGELICA

Candy young stems and leaf stalks in June, for decorating cakes and pastries. Cook small pieces with tart fruits to lessen acidity. Use to flavour jams, rhubarb and gooseberry, and fresh fruit salads. Boil stems or roots and eat as vegetable. Fresh leaves as tea for feverish colds. Dried leaves in pot-pourris and bath pochettes.

ANISE

Fresh young leaves in fruit and vegetable salads. The aromatic seeds (aniseeds) ground or whole used in fruit pies, cakes, biscuits, spiced breads and in drinks. Use with vegetables and meats and add to water when boiling fish. Ground seed as spice in pot-pourris.

BASIL

A strong spicy flavoured herb which adds a special piquancy to all tomato dishes, drinks, salads, sandwiches and soups. Use in ragout, pizza, omelettes and sprinkled sparingly over a green salad. Add to rice salad. A few chopped leaves mixed with salad oil is remedy for constipation.

BAY

Leaves, fresh, dried or crushed used as spicing agent in soups, stews, marinades and preserves. A necessary ingredient in bouquet garni – a bunch of herbs used to flavour foods cooked in liquid. Use crushed leaves in pot-pourris.

BERGAMOT, RED

Young fresh leaves and red flowers in salads. Good with pork. Add to Indian tea, wine or cocktails. Fresh or dried as tea, in hot milk as sedative. Dried leaves and flowers in pot-pourris and bath pochettes.

BORAGE

Flowers and very young leaves added to green salad. Flowers only in punches and wine cups or candied for sweets and decoration of cakes. Dried flowers add colour to pot-pourris. Fresh or dried leaves for refreshing iced tea – add touch of lemon or honey.

CARAWAY

Seeds are seasoning spice for cabbage, potatoes, dumplings, rich meats. Also in baking cakes and biscuits. Roots can be boiled as vegetable. An ingredient of Seed Tea used as digestive. Crushed seeds in pot-pourris.

CHAMOMILE

Flowers only used as tea – a good digestive after meals, as mouthwash for sore gums, as hair rinse for fair hair. Use as soothing eyebath, and in bath pochettes. Use in facial steam for relief of heavy cold. Flowers also in pot-pourris.

CHERVIL

Wonderful flavouring for soups, sauces and stews. Use generously. Combines well with other herbs in mixtures for omelettes and other egg and cheese dishes. Use in herb butter. As tea has a diuretic and blood-cleansing qualities.

CHIVES

Use in all foods and dishes requiring a mild onion flavour. Sprinkle them chopped on salads and soups and scrambled eggs. Try chives in place of onion in omelettes.

CORIANDER

Fresh leaves better known as 'Chinese Parsley'. Can be used in cooking in same manner as parsley. Use one or two crushed seeds to a small cup of coffee. Use whole or ground seed in cake baking, gingerbread, in baked or stewed apples and pears. Ground seed in home-made curry mixtures. Use in pot-pourris.

CORNFLOWER   Flowers only used fresh or dried. Add to other herbs to make infusion for soothing eyebath or compress. Dried flowers give colour to pot-pourris.

COSTMARY   Has strong minty flavour. Use tender young leaves for mint sauce. Use one or two leaves with veal or chicken. Add to apple jelly. Infusion makes a good refreshing tonic.

DILL   Use dill leaves for all fish and to flavour vegetables, salads and particularly cucumber. Use seed for pickling and spiced vinegars. Use as tea for hiccups and as digestive. Boil seeds in wine as sedative.

FENNEL   Traditional fish herb especially with oily fish. Add to salads, dressings for beetroot and carrot. Add to egg dishes. Leaves in facial pack good against freckles. Infusion for eyebath or compress, as skin cleanser. Fennel Seed Tea us digestive and diuretic for slimming.

GARLIC

Valuable flavouring in small amounts for all savoury foods; cut clove and rub on surface of food, round bowl or cooking pot.

HYSSOP

Add tender young leaves to vegetable salads and soups and to meat dishes. Try small amount in apricot pie. As tea it is a remedy for persistent cough and eases asthma.

LAVENDER

Use fresh or dried flowers in facial steams to improve complexion. Use in bath pochettes, lavender bags for linen. Important ingredient in pot-pourris and scented cushions.

LEMON BALM

Adds fragrant lemony mint flavour to chicken dishes, to jellies, ice-cream, fruit juices, wine cups, baked custard and fruit and vegetable salads. 'Melissa' tea is refreshing and relaxing. Ingredient in toilet water, pot-pourris and herb cushions.

LEMON VERBENA   Adds refreshing lemon taste to food and drinks such as fruit salads, herb jellies, fruit and wine cups. Fragrant tea hot or iced as sedative effect. Good scent in pot-pourris, sachets, herb cushions and soaps.

LOVAGE   Very good all-round herb for flavouring soups and stocks, adding its own 'meaty' strength. Sprinkle chopped fresh leaves over green salads. Use in bath pochettes; this stimulates skin and acts as deodorant. Infusion more like broth than tea, is diuretic and relaxing.

MARIGOLD   Dried or fresh petals in salads, egg, cheese and rice dishes. A colouring substitute for saffron. Use in baking cakes, custard, milk bread. Use in face compresses to clear skin. Soak petals in oil or ointment to heal skin blemishes. Use in pot-pourris.

MARJORAM   Add sweet marjoram to roast meats, poultry and game. Use with fish, tomatoes, mushrooms, potatoes and in rice dishes. Add to herb mixtures for stuffing and preserved meats. Soak leaves in oil to ease sprains and bruises. Marjoram tea stimulates the appetite.

Pot marjoram has a mild flavour, can be used in similar manner. Use dried leaves of both marjorams in pot-pourris and herb cushions.

MINT

Apart from traditional uses, good with young vegetables, cooked fruits and fruit salads, mint sorbet, peppermint ice-cream, fruit and wine cups. Use mint and peppermint tea as a refreshing digestive. Eau de Cologne mint and peppermint used in bath pochettes, herb sachets and pot-pourris.

NASTURTIUM

Good peppery seasoning for salad dressings and cream cheese. Leaves and flowers in green salads. Seeds substitute for capers. Dried flowers used with other herbs in skin cleansing facial steam and in pot-pourris.

PARSLEY

Indispensable for every kind of savoury food and as garnish. Roots of Hamburg parsley provide nutritious winter vegetable. Use leaf tea as diuretic tonic and for easing piles.

ROSE GERANIUM

Leaves add delicate sweet flavour to all fruit, home-made jams and jellies. Use in fruit and wine cups, with ice-cream and lemonade. Essential ingredient of pot-pourris, herb cushions and sachets.

ROSEMARY

Use to flavour both savoury and sweet dishes. Use with meat and vegetables, in risotto, omelettes and pancakes. Try ground rosemary in a biscuit mix, in herb butter, jellies and in herb vinegar for marinades. Use infusion as hair tonic for dark hair and skin lotion. Add to bath pochettes, herb cushions and pot-pourris.

SAGE

Strong herb, good with rich meats and oily fish. Traditional in onion stuffing. Try sage jelly with pork. Use leaves in fritters and savoury pancakes. Use in fruit drinks and apple juice. Infusion good for tightening skin, as hair tonic or rinse. Use in bath pochettes.

SALAD BURNET

An essential all-season salad herb as name implies. Gives flavour to other vegetables, stuffings, pork pie and sausages. Makes refreshing tea and flavours iced drinks. Soak compress in infusion for refining skin.

SAVORY
(Summer and Winter)

Summer savory has more delicate taste than winter variety. But they both bring out the flavour of all beans, fresh or dried, and greatly improve tinned and frozen beans. Good with other vegetables, in bean and pulse soups, with baked or poached fish, meat stews and spicy sauces.

SWEET CICELY

Less sugar needed with tart apples and other sour fruit if leafy sprig added to cooking pan. Use in green salads, herb butters and with all root vegetables. Add to water when cooking cabbage and cauliflower. Use in fruit salads, in trifles and custards and in plain whipped cream.

TARRAGON
(French)

Good culinary herb with most savoury foods, with poultry and mild vegetables such as asparagus, artichokes and courgettes. Use in herb butter, sauces, omelettes and other egg dishes.

THYME

Use with all meat, oily fish and most savoury foods and sauces. An ingredient of 'bouquet garni' – a bunch of herbs used to flavour foods cooked in liquid. Can be used in herb breads. Add lemon thyme to fruit salads, jellies and custards. Use infusion for soothing tired eyes. Tea is sedative and eases bronchitis. Use both thymes in bath pochettes, perfumes, soaps, herb cushions and pot-pourris.

VERBASCUM

Make tea from dried flowers only and strain well before drinking. Good for relieving persistent coughs or hoarseness, also bronchial colds. Use in pot-pourris to add colour.

WELSH ONION

Useful onion flavouring for cooking with all savoury foods. Easier to use than onion and not so strong. Perfect substitute for those who cannot normally digest onion.

Books in the Living with Herbs Series

An open-end series of beautiful paperbacks you can use in so many practical ways — written by leading herbalists and herb marketers. Each book contains four pages of full-color illustration, and many black and white drawings. Each volume is $2.50 per copy and they also come packaged in a 4-volume set ($10.00) for holiday gifts. Four titles in print now, with more to come.

At your nearest book, herbal supply or health store, or order direct from the publisher (postpaid).

Vol. 1 Herbs, Health and Astrology
by Leon Petulengro

A famous gypsy and noted astrologer records some of the ancient Romany beliefs about herbs and their links with astrology. Health patterns found in each of the Signs are discussed and the author offers specific remedies for various ailments based on *herbal astrological confluence.* Mr. Petulengro devotes an entire chapter to each Zodiac sign and a description of how the planets rule herbs. Includes many unusual recipes. $2.50

Vol. 2 Choosing, Planting and Cultivating Herbs
by Philippa Back

Herbs for city and country dweller, for gardeners who plan whole herb gardens and for those who may want to grow herbs in more modest surroundings — in window boxes, on balconies, in pots hung on trellises, or for other indoor pleasure. Philippa Back co-authored the famed *Herbs for Health* with Claire Loewenfeld. She includes an alphabetical listing of herbs as well as many garden plans and herb drawings. $2.50

Vol. 3 Growing Herbs as Aromatics
by Roy Genders

Here is told the history of pomanders, potpourris, scented waters, hanging baskets, rose perfumes and other uses of aromatics and spices. Best of all, the author shows how they can be grown and harvested, and includes a variety of ideas and recipes for their use today. Roy Genders' books include *A History of Scent, The Cottage Guide,* and *Scented Wild Flowers of Britain.* $2.50

Vol. 4 Making Things with Herbs
by Elizabeth Walker

Professional help for using herbs to make gifts, practical and frivolous, to adorn and embellish the house. Sachets, sweet bags, herbal teas, herbal essences, herb sacks for the kitchen, toys stuffed with herbs, and all kinds of other delights become so easy with Ms. Walker's practical expert advice. The author's experience comes from running a very active family business called "Meadow Herbs" in England, which makes and markets herb products. $2.50

The *Living with Herbs* Series is published by
Keats Publishing, Inc., New Canaan, Connecticut, 06840.

Other Related-Interest Books You Will Enjoy

*Ask for them at your nearest book or health store
or order direct from the publisher.*

Nature's Big, Beautiful, Bountiful Feel-Good Book
Selected by the editors of The Health Quarterly,
Nutritional Update and Healthful Living Today

A veritable Whole Earth Catalog of health featuring articles, presentations, interviews with more than seventy leading doctors, researchers and specialists in health and consumerism. Includes the latest on prevention and cure of illness; gardening tips, recipes, reference information; poetry; cartoons; reviews of 100 best books on health — in a big, lavishly illustrated book. Hardcover $11.95. Paperback $6.95.

Eat the Weeds
by Ben Charles Harris

The famous classic about all the "free" things to eat for better health by one of America's leading herbalists. Paperback $1.50

Plants, Flowers and Herbs of the Bible
by W. E. Shewell-Cooper

One of the leading British horticulturists and organic gardening specialists brings together all the plants, flowers, fruits and herbs mentioned in the Bible. Hardcover $7.95. Paperback $3.95.

Good Food, Naturally
by John B. Harrison

The author believes that the organic method of farming is a method that enriches the soil and ensures productive use years from now. A how-to book based on explanations of how soil, plants and animals interact. Hardcover $4.95. Paperback $3.95.

My Secrets of Natural Beauty
by Virginia Castleton Thomas

In a unique handbook of beauty care, using natural ingredients, the author reveals formulas of famous women from Cleopatra on. Chapters on nutrition, diet and exercise. Hardcover $5.95. Paperback $2.95.

Loaves and Fishes
by Malvina Kinard & Janet Crisler

Drawing on their combined experience in archaeological research, biblical study, and in professional cookery, the authors have reconstructed a culinary monument — more than 150 dishes based on Bible foods or today's equivalents. Hardcover $8.95.

Add a Few Sprouts
by Martha H. Oliver

This book explains as well as instructs, and offers a selection of sprout recipes suitable for all courses of a meal. Paperback $1.50

Keats Publishing, Inc., New Canaan, Connecticut, 06840.